When Two Become One:

A Transparent Journey into the Foundation of Our Marriage

MARCUS AND TEISHA FRIEND

Copyright (c) 2025 Marcus & Teisha Friend.
All rights are reserved. No part of this work may be reproduced, stored in a retrieval system, or transmitted in any form or by any means, electronic, electrical, chemical, mechanical, optical, photocopying, recording, or otherwise, without the author's and copyright owner's prior written permission.
ISBN: 9798303103818

TABLE OF CONTENTS

Acknowledgements	4
Welcome	6
Introduction	8
Memory One	10
Memory Two	17
Memory Three	26
Memory Four	35
Memory Five	45
Memory Six	54
Memory Seven	63
Memory Eight	71
Memory Nine	80
Memory Ten	91

ACKNOWLEDGEMENTS

Teisha and Marcus, AKA #TEAMFRIEND, thank God for His saving grace and keeping power. We know, beyond a shadow of a doubt, that it is in Him, we live, move, and have our being. Our gratitude for our existence, life, marriage, family, calling, and journey will forever be expressed in our daily living for God our Father, Jesus our Lord and Savior, and the Holy Spirit our companion and comforter. We would also like to thank all of you who have graciously supported our marriage and ministry in any capacity over the years.

We want to give special thanks to Mike and Karmel Pope, founders and facilitators of *Marriage More Abundantly Couple's Ministry*, for all that you and *Marriage More* have poured into us over the years. You have compassionately been a safe place for us to be transparent and free in a no-judgment zone. Without you, this book and our marriage would not be the same or even exist. We love our *Marriage More* family!

We cannot mention the individual names of those we want to acknowledge. However, we want to thank a particular individual, Ms.Tearie Leslie, who has not only supported us tremendously throughout our marriage but was the first to suggest that we should write a book. She indicated that in the comment posted below, and months later, she looked at us and asked in a gentle yet piercing tone, "When are y'all gonna write that book?" After being asked, "What book?" she responded ever so charmingly with her signature warm smile, "You know what book."

Ms. Tearie, we are grateful for you as a person, as a babysitter, as a listening ear, as a voice of wisdom, as a constant pillar of strength, encouragement, and support, and finally, as a significant inspiration as to why we can share our story with the world in this magnitude. Our love for you is endless.

WE WELCOME YOU!

Welcome to our love story! Our journey comprised a conglomerate of experiences–good, bad, and indifferent–
that made us who we are today- #teamfriend. We will be very transparent as we attempt to share precious and meaningful pieces of our relationship and marital puzzle.

This book is by no means a "blueprint," if you will, but we certainly pray that it will offer inspiration and hope in a relatable and attainable way. Our relationship/ marriage is ours, and yours is yours; however, we have discovered that most, if not all, relationships encounter very similar challenges in certain areas. Those include but are not limited to communication, family, past choices, working together, commitment, determination in demanding times, attaining a support system, implementing problem-solving tactics, selecting those who you can trust to speak into your lives, and many more. Our hearts desire to encourage each reader, and we pray that you will be better after experiencing a walk-through of our open house of testimonies and lessons.

We realize we have not arrived at perfection, but our journey toward it is getting better, easier, and more enjoyable! We are grateful that we have grown, learned, and loved, all while being humble enough to acknowledge that we are #stillgrowing, #stillloving, and #stilllearning- and we will forever be as long as we are two becoming one! We thank you, and we love you!

INTRODUCTION:
How We Birthed this Book

As we approached our 10th wedding anniversary, we had an intriguing idea that we agreed to pursue that would be a blessing to others as much as it would to us. We decided to have an "All White Affair" anniversary party where we would invite several couples we knew who had touched our marriage along the way. We chose specific couples to encourage the attendees on preassigned topics. We had a host of friends, tasty food, a live saxophonist, a beautiful backdrop alongside a small lake, a lovely ambiance, soulful dancing, and an overall flawless evening of celebration. Conversations still float around about that awesome gathering and how fun and encouraging it was.

Leading up to that September day in 2017, we decided to plant some seeds that we did not know would eventually sprout into what you hold in your hand at this very moment. We each posted one memory per person daily on social media for ten consecutive days, starting 10 days before the anniversary party. We branded our entries "#countdownto10." These memories reflected monumental moments throughout our dating relationship and our marriage.

Transparency was key as we highlighted several memorable occasions that contributed mightily to our foundation and our growth as a couple. We, by the grace of God, now share those with you. We pray that you are encouraged, inspired, uplifted, strengthened, challenged, and changed for the better after absorbing our firsthand experiences. Blessings to you!

Memory One

For the next couple of days, Marcus Friend and I will share some of our personal journey to 10 years...it's no secret how much we love each other but it has ALWAYS been our passion to encourage fun, genuine, God ordained marriages! When I see these photos I smile(my dimples are definitely showing) and love how at ANY moment we can be smooth and the next we look like Bonnie and Clyde...i love this Man of God
#we2b14ever #friends4ever

Teisha's Takeaway

Making memories and having photos have been vital in overcoming the growing pains of becoming one. Being able to have memories of reflections has encouraged me to keep pushing and to keep going, knowing this will get better. Creating memories provides a positive image and inspiration, the spark that reminds me of why I said, "I do," rather than an unproductive thought that says, "I can't."

Marcus's Takeaway

As I reflect on the various photos, attire, and environments displayed, I think about how, no matter what, we must collaborate to maintain true happiness in our marriage. No matter what happens, we must be determined to stand not just "with" but also "for" our spouse to overcome life's obstacles and still emerge with genuine smiles and laughter on the other side of the challenges.

Our Takeaway

Making memories is important because they serve many purposes. For one, they can be monuments to remind us of where we have come from and motivate us to keep moving forward. They also serve as memorials to mark our progress. Lastly, they inspire us to persist in pushing through the walls of resistance and remain joyful as we encounter future marital opposition. #wegrewhere

Your Takeaway

"Absolutely! God is always first!!!"

—Susan Walls

Marcus Friend
August 17, 2017

1. I remember watching her dad escort my BEAUTIFUL bride as they took the scenic route over the river and through the woods of the greenery and garden of Antebellum House. As she approached the altar, I was so excited to be the groom of such a pretty girl. I thank God for trusting me with His daughter. #countdownto10

Marcus's Takeaway

Teisha has always been a beautiful woman to me. Obviously, the outside is not the complete person, as we are all comprised of body, soul, and spirit. However, on September 2, 2007, at 5 o'clock in the evening, as her dad ushered her along the path that eventually brought her to the altar, I seemed only to be able to focus on the beauty and aesthetic pleasure radiating from her gorgeous, melanated, honey-glazed brown skin accented by her bright smile. That girl, my girl, made my eyes beat in the same rhythmic pattern as my heart. She remains as beautiful today as she did the day her father delivered her to me before God and the attendees who witnessed our wedding ceremony. I remain as grateful today as I was then. I still thank God for this priceless jewel He packaged as an illustrious and splendid soul encapsulated in an amazingly attractive enclosure of skin that is forever easy on my eyes. True beauty is not just on the outside, but the part that *IS* on the outside sure helps! I genuinely believe God showed me how much He really loves me by allowing me to find my wife–His daughter–that He reserved for me.

Teisha's Takeaway

Reflecting on this memory from Marcus, I am reminded to see myself as a beautiful daughter of God. Oftentimes, I would feel discouraged and unworthy of being loved. I have made many mistakes and wrong decisions, yet Marcus (and my father) loves me anyhow. Like my heavenly father, Marcus knew my vulnerabilities and still took the scenic route with me. That is a memory I will forever cherish. I am fully known and loved by you!

Our Takeaway

Although we are often captivated by the outside, we do not always know what someone is going through on the inside. Like the adage, "Beauty is only skin deep," we must be able to deal with the internal struggles of our spouses for the marriage to be successful. When we do that, it strengthens the whole individual, which in turn nourishes the relationship between the two. It helps to know that your spouse is beautiful/handsome, but wisdom says to go deeper and embrace the totality of your spouse to discover the inner beauty they possess as well. In doing so, we will also unveil our responsibilities (as husbands) to cover and (as wives) to undergird our spouses in prayer and life. #stilllearning

*DISCLAIMER: God made male and female. We base our thoughts and opinions on His promises according to His order in His Word.

Your Takeaway

_____

_____

_____

_____

_____

_____

_____

_____

_____

_____

_____

_____

_____

_____

_____

_____

_____

_____

"I LOVE THIS COUPLE!"
–Joseph Merrell

Memory Two

Teisha Fletcher-Friend is with **Emma Vines**.
August 18, 2017

Another memory from 10 years with **Marcus Friend**...
One year we went on a retreat with some friends..during the retreat Marcus and I went Jet Skiing on the lake. Because we were young and in love neither of us worried about the fact we couldn't swim...until we flipped over! After being rescued by a Rescue Diver and returning to our room we began arguing about who was to blame....later that evening one of our friends ministered to us a Vision and a Word from the Lord that remains with us, "The power of our Words."
Although we can Now laugh at that incident, it's more important to understande the importance of surrounding yourself with people who pour Truth in you. Thank you to all who has been influential in our growth as a couple...and NO it wasn't my fault~i just leaned a little bit😊

Teisha's Takeaway

    This memory was so powerful because it reminded me of the foundational principles of a healthy marriage. Communication is a word we heard numerous times throughout marital counseling and advice from other married couples. Scripture even teaches that out of the abundance of the heart, the mouth speaks, and boy, my mouth revealed what was in my heart. I had a spirit of competition rather than a spirit of oneness. My motivation in discussions was to be correct and heard rather than how to resolve our issue best. I was so determined not to be the blame that I was willing to cut Marcus with my words. I was even taking score as if I were in battle against Marcus instead of being in union with Marcus. I was winning, but WE were losing—WOW! This memory reminds me of how crucial it is to be grounded in the Word. When I am distressed, I am reminded of the importance of having God's Word in my heart and pulling on the Word rather than my flesh. As always, God is our help in times of need. That rescue diver, our minister friends, and, most importantly, the Word brought us our deliverance. This is the memory where I can honestly say we have trusted God to deliver us, not just out of a situation but from ourselves. Learning how to communicate in challenging times has been one of my prized possessions.

Marcus's Takeaway

This memory has numerous takeaways, but I will not discuss them all right now. Much of what happened in the jet skiing incident pointed directly to our inability to communicate and work together to prevent the issue and, more importantly, the initial issue from growing into a much bigger one. On the other hand, I learned that even during potential disasters, God can and will have people in the right positions to keep you afloat when you are sinking! The guy who "happened to sail by" on a party boat while we struggled to reposition and remount the jet ski was a certified and trained deep sea vessel recovery technician. Go figure! He helped safely get us and the inoperable, sinking jet ski to shore. He then disappeared without giving us info to contact or compensate him, although we had asked more than once. Later, as stated in the memory, our friends and co-laborers in the ministry gave us a Word that opened our eyes to the power of our words and how we were tearing one another down by playing the blame game. This experience taught me that it is always good to have people around whom you can trust to help you. (We will discuss this more in my memory #5). Another takeaway I will mention is that amid turmoil, there are always positives that can help you if you are open to growing and learning. Not every situation with less than your desired outcome must be viewed negatively. There is typically a positive nugget to take with you. Even a broken clock is right twice a day!

Our Takeaway

God has a way of showing us where we really are, especially when we think we are further along than we are. This memory surely called for introspection. We both had to own our part in the breakdown (no pun intended). We also learned to appreciate the good amid what appears to be bad. It is much easier to move forward together when we acknowledge and grasp the building blocks, no matter how small, and use those to construct faith and optimism for our future. It is critical to assess your circle to make sure you have people around you to hold you accountable. No matter how grand the bow is, an arrow with no direction will miss its target every time. Likewise, a lovely house, fine cars, fancy clothes, public smiles, and even some children will lead to misery and dysfunction without the proper communication foundation and boundaries to help keep us focused when distractions come. We must humbly keep a mindset that allows growth and development in our marriage. #stillgrowing

Your Takeaway

_____

_____

_____

_____

_____

_____

_____

_____

_____

_____

_____

_____

_____

_____

_____

_____

_____

_____

> "This is so nice. I really had given up on relationships, but this gives me hope. Y'all keep doing what you are doing in sharing your stories- you never know who might need to hear them."
> ~Ersula Adams

Marcus Friend
August 18, 2017

So here's my second memory of our #countdownto10 2. I remember the night of the wedding. We were both EXHAUSTED! We laughed, talked, reminisced, rejoiced, looked in each others eyes, talked about the wedding, our future, the honeymoon, etc. We were ONE! We were so excited about our marriage. We were pleased. We were looking forward to what God had in store for us. We made sure we had everything packed. We smiled. We were overjoyed. We felt like everything was complete. We were taking it all in. Next thing I know I woke up at like 3 in the morning with one eye open like...wait, did we consummate??

Marcus's Takeaway

With all the hustle and bustle of life, it is mandatory to maintain order and prioritize what is important. We can get so busy working, coaching, cooking, volunteering, spending time with family, running children to appointments, practices, and games, paying bills, cleaning the house, grocery shopping, going to church, etc., that we miss taking time out to spend with each other. Although all the aforementioned responsibilities are necessary, we must remember that our spouse needs and desires intimate quality time with us. In a marriage, that time is like the water in God's nuptial tank, which causes us to stay afloat. That intimacy (not always sexual) provides the connection that causes us to know each other beyond the flesh. It allows us to tie into one another so firmly that we cannot tell where one's hooks end and the others begin. That is symbolic of the two becoming one. Keep the main thing the main thing!

Teisha's Takeaway

We really ended the night with a bang! We were so exhausted from celebrating and excited to start our lives together that all we could do was sleep. LOL, boy, I was glad that Marcus understood. Yes, we had other plans, but our bodies were worn out. If nothing else, we learned how to be understanding and flexible. We may have missed intimacy the first night, but we knew we had forever to make up for it. Knowing that fireworks were the expectation for the night, I should have planned accordingly. The busyness of life, although needed, often becomes a distraction from the more pertinent things. Create boundaries and recognize when you are treading close to the edge. Be intentional about meeting the needs of your spouse.

Our Takeaway

We must keep our spouse's needs and wants at the forefront of our minds. We must "do life" and simultaneously prioritize our marital necessities for a flourishing marriage. A high school football coach once said that *BALANCE* was the most important seven-letter word in the English vocabulary. With that in mind, we have realized that a healthy dose of intimacy keeps the scales in our favor. The Bible says in Proverbs 4:7, in the B part of the verse, "In all thy getting, get an understanding." We like to think that if there were a bible for marriages, it would say, "In all your time, get you some intimate quality time." Let the married church say, "AMEN!" #stillloving

Your Takeaway

"I just leaned a little bit!" Lol
#ilovetheFriends
~ Natasha Wilson

Memory Three

Teisha Fletcher-Friend
August 19, 2017

Memory #3 with Marcus Friend..
I remember having trouble early in the relationship becoming one~specifically regarding finances. Marcus made good money. I made good money. We both paid our bills on time...we were good except I was uncomfortable bringing our finances together. What's really odd is that Marcus was and is hands down better with money and had more than proven himself trustworthy...but I was still shaking! I asked God to help me in this area because I knew it was something holding me back....needless to say we are definitely stronger as One...in fact I can genuinely say, "I trust his every decision!" I reflect on Marcus telling me, "Stick with me and I'll show you some things!"
#we2b14ever #2friends #growing2gether #countdownto10

Teisha's Takeaway

Trust issues in a relationship can show up in several ways, and for me, it was here—in the finances. I was okay with my account, your account, and our account. The trust issues began to surface with the "our account." The struggle went against what I had heard for years: "Don't put all your eggs in one basket.... You better keep a stash for a rainy day." My faith and what I had been taught in my upbringing were indeed a struggle. It was here where I chose to walk in faith. I decided that I would trust God to lead Marcus in our finances, and boy, was this a faith walk. This was not about Marcus's ability to be financially responsible but rather about me releasing control and trusting God. I remember feeling so vulnerable. I asked Marcus to be transparent about every dollar spent to ease my concerns and to prove his trustworthiness. Boy, I am thankful that Marcus was patient and understanding as we established our financial bridge of trust.

Marcus's Takeaway

I am ever so grateful that God, through some people of wisdom and through some tough times, taught me the value of money and how and why to be responsible with it. I want my wife to trust me in every area, and an effective way to welcome that trust is to show accountability and responsibility for our resources. I am conservative, so not splurging comes easily. However, the other side is knowing when to spend, save, invest, etc. I thank God for what we have accomplished financially over the years. Were there a couple of mistakes and not-so-good decisions? In hindsight, yes, but we made it through. This Godly aspect of managing our finances has also contributed to us having a stronger bond and a deeper trust in one another. As a result of His leading me and showing me how to lead my wife and family, she is still sticking with me, and I am still showing her some things. To God be the glory. #stillgrowing

Our Takeaway

One area that can either cause a strain or strengthen a marriage is finances. Whether you are prudent or a lavish spender, there is an opportunity to grow and to learn how to find a healthy balance. Both parties face moments challenging their abilities to trust the other spouse's decision-making. How each spouse manages funds typically indicates problems arising (or not) in other areas of the marriage. For instance, liberal, impulsive spenders will have fewer resources for vacations, date nights, getaways, etc.

Sometimes, they may even splurge on a vacation but then come home to overdue bills and do not have the resources to pay them. Boy, can that open doors for concern, stress, and even arguments. Meanwhile, more frugal, economical money managers will have something saved to enjoy some special occasions without going into debt. This leaves both parties confident, reassured, secure in their finances, and peaceful in other areas of the marriage. Either way, we must understand that when the two become one, financial decisions for both are crucial to the joy and comfortability of the union.

Your Takeaway

_____

_____

_____

_____

_____

_____

_____

_____

_____

_____

_____

_____

_____

_____

_____

_____

_____

_____

_____

"God's way is ALWAYS the right way.
Equally yoked and prosperous!
So proud of y'all."
~April M Briggs

Marcus Friend
August 21, 2017

This is my memory # 3 in our #countdownto10: I remember one day earlier in our marriage, I got up on my off day (which I had emphasized several times that on my OFF day, I'm OFF), went out in the hot sun and meticulously mowed the lawn, edged it, did the weedeating, cut a tree down, cut it into small limbs and dragged it to the side of the street to be picked up. As the elders say "I was fit to be tired!" I went in the house and ran some dish water to wash the dishes. About that time Teisha came home from work. She came in through the garage into the kitchen. Without a greeting, a hug, a kiss or anything, she looked and blurted out "Awww Marcus, you haven't washed the dishes?" At that point, that day became known as "the day we came off of our honeymoon!" I looked at Teisha and gave her a very detailed explanation of EVERY THING that I HAD done that day. We ended up talking about it and we grew that day. We learned that we should acknowledge what each other does before we criticize or complain about what has NOT been done. We learned to ask before we assume. We learned that the APPROACH to a conversation makes all the difference in dictating the course of said conversation. We greet each other with a kiss on sight every time we enter each other's presence. We learned that a soft answer turns away wrath (Proverbs 15:1). We learned. We continue to learn. We loved. We continue to love. #countdownto10 #teamFriend— with **Teisha Fletcher-Friend**.

Marcus's Takeaway

Being married can be very humbling at times. Just when you think you have earned some "good jobs," pats on the back, and some "at-a-boys," you better realize that your motives and expectations must be pure. I really wanted Teisha to acknowledge all my hard work, but she happened to stroll into the garage without seeing the fruits of my labor. Yes, I feel like there was no way she could overlook that beautiful yard, especially with a tree cut down, but I somehow saw the dishes in the sink that I was about to wash (at that)! The big pile of limbs by the driveway at the ditch would be a dead giveaway.... LOL. However, even though I was upset by her oversight, I should not have "come off of the honeymoon." I could have CALMLY stated that I had not been lying in bed with the remote all day and explained my daily accomplishments without giving her the encyclopedia's detailed version. We REALLY grew that day through communication and seeking to understand rather than be understood. Thank God for grace! #stilllearning

Teisha's Takeaway

What a memory! Oh, how I remember this day so vividly. I was so consumed with my needs and wants that I painfully overlooked Marcus's hard work and accomplishments. His needs are just as important as mine. This was the day I became more intentional about focusing on the pros rather than the cons. It does not mean I do not see them (areas that need addressing). It simply means I choose to focus on the good first. This approach has made having tough conversations easier by softening my approach regarding the cons. I sure do hate that this is what brought us off our honeymoon. If a lesson were to be learned, I learned it that day. My husband is more than someone who completes my honey-do list. He is my partner and teammate who should hear, "Thank you, I appreciate your work, great job, and I'm so proud of you" more often.

Our Takeaway

In life, we often effortlessly see what is important to us. In marriage, however, we must focus on what is important to our spouses. A selfless marriage is a successful marriage because the goal is to please the other in every area. That forces us to take note of and prioritize their needs and wants over our own. When we do that, we cannot help but give affirmations and applause for the accomplishments of the other because we are tuned in to what is significant to them. Even when we miss it, communication is key. Not just knowing what to say but how to say it. Reconciliation is a powerful tool in marriage. We do not ever want the sun to go down on our wrath. We must be intentional about making our spouse's needs a preference.

Your Takeaway

"We can relate. Thanks for sharing!!!!"
#THEBRUCES!#

36

Memory Four

Memory #4...one evening during our courtship Marcus Friend came over and helped me take out some braids..while doing so Marcus asked about my relationship with my dad..I gave him my usual response when ever asked about him, "We don't have one. I hadn't had one with him and have learned to manage pretty well." To my surprise, he asked more questions and exposed years of pain that I didn't know existed. After exposing my true feelings, Marcus began to minister about how Christ Jesus has forgiven us...Long story short, my heart was beginning to heal and I made the first step towards forgiving my dad. Marcus doesn't just minister behind the pulpit but he ministers wherever he is!
#meandmydad #ministrystartsathome #countdownto10

Teisha's Takeaway

    This was certainly not the conversation I was hoping to have that night. It was supposed to end after I gave my answer about our relationship. Never had anyone cared enough to start peeling the layers of pain. Marcus allowed me the space to express my hurt and my pain in the years of failed and/or unmet expectations from my dad. This is where we *yada* one another. This is where we become intimate with one another, like the woman at the well (John 4). God used Marcus to begin ministering to an area where I was bruised. This was crucial because if I did not heal, I could only love Marcus from a place of hurt. It's funny how a night of taking my braids out was the beginning of tearing down a wall of abandonment to build a lifestyle of commitment. This memory serves as a reminder of the importance of having a spouse who cares for your soul just as they care for your heart.

Marcus's Takeaway

It is incredible what simple conversation can sometimes unveil. I asked Teisha about her relationship with her father because fathers usually set the pattern for how their daughters see men, especially in adulthood. I did not know I was scratching the scab off a hidden wound. I knew unforgiveness only hurts the one who harbors it, and there was a lot for her to unload. I have long been a believer in John 13:34-35. If God can (and He does) forgive and love us after all we have done against His will, surely, we can forgive and love those who have wronged us. That revelation escorted Teisha to do what her heart knew was right, but she did not know *how* to do it. I cared about her enough to want her healed, whole, and right in the eyes of God, whether we ever survived as a couple or not. Our priority is God first, then us.

Our Takeaway

This memory serves as one that exposed way more than what was on the surface. The conversation about the father/daughter relationship revealed years of pain and disappointment. What also came to light was our desire to be equally yoked and on one accord as it pertained to us taking our spiritual walks seriously. It would have been easy to say, "Yeah, that's messed up how you all's relationship is," just change the subject and keep it moving.

Instead, the heart and love of God were reflected by consistent efforts to get the healing process started. At the same time, the seriousness of a relationship with God was noticeable in how the Word was embraced and applied to the situation. Seeing the honest intent of each other's willingness to please God contributed mightily to our spiritual oneness with Him and each other. It sure does the marriage good to know we have each other's back in the spirit realm and the natural.... And to think, this all started with a conversation while taking some braids down. Our God is so amazing!

Your Takeaway

"Thank you for allowing us to share in your journey to becoming the awesome couple that you are. Thank you for being a role model to others. Wishing you many more years of happiness...Luv ya both!"
~Letetia Johnson

Marcus Friend
August 22, 2017

Memory # 4 of the #countdownto10 : I remember when I first met Teisha's dad. The three of us met at Mama Annies restaurant, who btw catered our wedding and will be catering our 10th anniversary celebration/party (I need to charge them an advertising fee!). We talked for a couple of hours or so. The one thing that stuck out most to me was when her dad looked me square in the eyes and in a semi-threatening tone said "Whatever you do, don't hurt her." I thought "Wow!" I guess that's what a dad is supposed to say in front of his daughter to let her know he has her back! Funny thing was he didn't know I had been helping her to heal from the devastating pain and untapped issues festering in her heart that were caused by none other than who...him, her dad, her covering, her backbone, her safety net, her encourager, her counselor, her motivator, her protector, her sounding board, her constant reminder of how great she is, the one who would always be there in her corner as long as he could, her father, her forever fan----well supposedly anyway. Lesson, sometimes we hurt deeply the very ones we are supposed to help mightily! We sometimes ignorantly bring the most pain while warning everyone else to tread lightly on the tender heart that we have torn to pieces. I've never raised one finger to hit or hurt my wife. I have, however, said things to hurt her emotionally. When I did, I apologized and got it right- with her AND God. As we continue this journey through life as husband and wife, I explore the things that hurt her and make every attempt to avoid them. The last thing that I want to do is stomp on the heart (or emotions) that God sent me to protect and bless. Still learning, still growing, still loving... #countdownto10 #teamFriend— with **Teisha Fletcher-Friend**.

Marcus's Takeaway

It was so ironic to hear the person responsible for deeply hurting Teisha "warn" me not to hurt her. I could not corral the confusion that was running around in my mind. It was my first time meeting him, so I did not know the best response. I know what I was thinking about saying would not fare well for him and me moving forward. I didn't want my relationship with my future father-in-law to be a one-day affair, so I digressed and responded with a simple, "I won't." All the while, I am thinking, "He must not know the damage he has caused her, much less that I am the one trying to repair the heart that he broke." I learned from that encounter that I never wanted to be as delusional as I saw him being. I would never demand that my wife be respected while I disrespect her. I cannot teach our children to always care for her if I demonstrate a careless attitude towards her. I cannot request anyone to love, forgive, or have patience with her if I do not first be an example. I may not have liked the road her dad led me on to get there, but I can certainly appreciate the sobering destination of reality where I arrived. If I expect specific behavior towards her from others, she can surely expect them from me first.

Teisha's Takeaway

I'm unsure if I was around when this conversation occurred, but I'm guessing I wasn't, or I was further along in my healing process than I can remember. However, reflecting on this memory, I can only think about my dad's good intentions. Unfortunately, good intentions can only go so far; at some point, our actions must align with those thoughts. My dad's intentions stood alone at the restaurant, but good intentions must be coupled with corresponding actions. That can be easier said than done, but with sacrifice, it is possible. I want my husband and family to know I love them, not just because I say it but because I show it in their love language. This memory encourages me to reflect on my actions concerning my marriage. I intentionally demonstrate behaviors that strengthen our bond rather than cause detrimental damage to the one I love.

Our Takeaway

We must be careful and intentional about practicing what we preach. When we do not, we can be model hypocrites on display. It is pertinent that we demonstrate the behavior that we communicate. Even when we "really mean" something, we must convey the same to the recipient. It is a healthy habit to ask your spouse occasionally, "Are my actions measured up to my words?" Hear their response clearly and thoroughly without offense so you can contribute what they need from you (refer to our takeaway from memory #3). Stay in a position where you can communicate openly and freely, without reservation, about whether or not your character lines up with your words. Remember the adage: "Actions speak louder than words." Whatever you say you are to and/or for your spouse, stand on it!

Your Takeaway

"Sometimes we harbor unspeakable heartfelt pain. Then, God in His infinite wisdom sends "His Cardiologist" to ease the hurt. You two were purposely fashioned by God just for each other. You both are superb examples of God's matchless love for those that have learned and continue to learn how to lean on Jesus. I sincerely salute you Friendly Ministers."
~Adrienne Jamison

47

Memory Five

Teisha Fletcher-Friend
August 23, 2017

Strolling down Memory Lane with Marcus Friend..#5
I remember first seeing Marcus at the 📖 and thinking he was nice looking but after seeing a booster seat in his car I thought, "Not interested!" My checklist for dating NEVER included someone with kids. My motto was,"You don't have to share me and I shouldn't have to share you" (and of course No Baby Mama Drama). Sooooo after giving into Marcus handsome face, charming personality, and his passion for Christ(yep, He sold me his cd, Here It Is)I decided to give him my number. During each of our dates Marcus made it clear to me how much Mariun meant to him. He was more than a weekend dad~he was involved and I was going to have to share....hum, was I selfish? This was going to be an opportunity for me to grow~was I ready? 10 years later I'm still thanking God for the growth. I can't believe I almost missed my blessing because I wanted it to be "All about me!" Lesson: Having a check list is good but trusting God is better! Scripture teaches us that thou we make plans, it is the Lord's way that prevails.
#lovemyBonusbaby #countdownto10 #we2b14ever

Teisha's Takeaway

    This one memory makes me smile and praise God all at once. Boy, I almost missed one of the best blessings I didn't ask for. As the memory states, a checklist is good, but trusting God is better! God had preordained us way before we were born. His thoughts and ways are higher and far better than ours any day! This memory is an encouragement to trust God's plan for you. Your prosperous ways and good health are all locked into God's way and God's plan. Do not be misguided because they do not come

48

packaged as you think they should. Be careful not to forsake the one who will bring you into your promised land. You must hearken unto the voice of God rather than others or even yourself. The cologne smelled great, and his face was stunning, but the car seat brought about my growth.

Marcus's Takeaway

I did not know until a good while later that the booster seat in my car had initially turned Teisha off. When I did find out, I was bothered because I knew I was not going to forsake my son for a woman I was interested in. Mariun and I were a package deal. Fast forward a few years, and the funny thing is Teisha encouraged and supported me wholeheartedly as I/we eventually obtained full-time custody of Mariun! I am glad that I held to my standards and that she changed her heart from her original thoughts. We progressed by adding two more sons to be one big happy family.

Our Takeaway

There is nothing wrong with having convictions or even a "list" of things you want and don't want in a spouse. We must accept that when our list does not align with what He has for us, it will do us well to submit to His better judgment. We know a woman determined that her husband would be over six feet tall, have a dark complexion, athletic build, and so on. Years later, she is still single. There is no shade towards her; it is just that we must give God room to bring us who He has for us and not get caught up in what we see and want instead. Mariun was and is the best son we could have ever dreamed of...and to think we almost missed this experience because of a list! Proverbs 19:21 teaches us there are many plans in a man's heart, but the Lord's purpose will prevail.

Your Takeaway

_____

_____

_____

_____

_____

_____

_____

_____

_____

_____

_____

_____

_____

_____

_____

_____

_____

_____

_____

"I'm just cracking up... that's good stuff! Just wait ...there's more to come! Your transparency in marriage, as you both share triumphs over trials, is a blessing. Marriage is a Ministry! So glad you're in it! Continual blessings over you both!"
`Eloise Agee Williams

Marcus Friend
August 24, 2017

My memory #5 in our #countdownto10 : When Teisha Fletcher-Friend and I were dating, we talked about marriages of longevity in our respective families. Though my biological mom and dad were separated as far back as I can remember and eventually divorced, my dad and bonus mom at that time had about 25 years of marriage under their belts. Teisha, as we talked about it, realized that no one on her side had a sustained marriage for very long that could serve as a model. We came to the conclusion that we HAD to depend on GOD! We couldn't allow single experts to sow into our marital advice garden. Any and everybody don't get to speak into our lives/marraige. We have had our share of ups and downs and challenges. However, the Spirit of God has kept us through every valley and on every hill. We learned who to LISTEN to and who to "just let talk". At the end of the day He has kept us! We are yet learning, yet growing and yet loving. #countdownto10 #teamFriend

Marcus's Takeaway

It is good to have people close to you who you can connect with and who have been where you are trying to go. Their experiences can benefit you even if, at times, you must "eat the fish and spit out the bones." When you are chartering unfamiliar territory, have no predecessor to call upon, and no one familiar with the course, God is always the perfect guide. He will lead flawed people flawlessly to the destination He desires. If you have never trusted God, you will discover even more undeveloped paths; trusting is a mandate in marriage! When it seems like there is no groundbreaker, follow the One who made the ground. He laid the foundation for marriage.

Teisha's Takeaway

I had members of my family who had been married, but no one had remained married. I wanted not only to be married but to remain happily married. I knew this was going to require me to put in some work. I looked over my upbringing, evaluated what I knew about marriage, and decided I would do everything contrary to what I had witnessed in other marriages. I put my complete faith in God rather than the advice of friends and family. There were many times I felt isolated and alone, but I was reminded that I wanted something different. Dave Ramsey has this saying, "If you would live like no one else, later you can live like no one else," and I took that to the field and worked on my marriage. I surrounded myself with Godly wisdom and took heed to the happily married couples. Marcus and I became intentional about our goals for our marriage. By the grace of God, we are still married, happy, and growing.

Our Takeaway

Most people want good examples of successful marriages from which they can glean. Besides Thomas and Shelia Friend's marriage, we did not have many models of wholesome unions. We did, however, have many examples of what we did not want. So, we chose to learn even from the negative, short-lived exhibits around us. We learned a lot about what not to incorporate while we remained focused on our goal of having a long-lasting, happy, and fulfilling marriage. Date nights, time alone, deep (and sometimes challenging) conversations, marriage groups (like *Marriage More' Abundantly* in Huntsville, Alabama), and frequent glances at your marital goals contribute to marital bliss. We depended heavily on God and our individual and corporate relationships with Him. Marriage reflects God's relationship with the Church (Ephesians 5:21-32). How can we reflect God's intent without Him being the focal point? We are like the two points at the bottom of a triangle, with God being the third point at the top; the more we move towards Him, the closer we get to one another. We learned that when you allow God to order your matrimonial steps, you may be the first in the family with a sustaining union, but be the example for those coming behind you.

Your Takeaway

"You have made me a better person just knowing you and I
know that there is still true love. God is with you always
and I am standing with you too."
~Sandy Hillis Steakley

Memory Six

 Teisha Fletcher-Friend is with **Marcus Friend**.
August 25, 2017

Countdown to 10 with Marcus Friend: memory #6
Though Marcus and I come from different backgrounds we both share an appreciation for where we are and what we have..I recall purchasing our first home together and not having anything but keys...we agreed we wouldn't go into any debt trying to decorate or furnish the house but instead we would do one room at a time...we even had a house warming party where guest had to B.Y.O.C.(bring your own chair)...we slept on a blow up mattress until we purchased our first bed~yep, just the bed~no bedroom suite! God is faithful and desires for us to be faithful to Him..as we embark on our new home we give God ALL glory...though we will have twice as many rooms we can say there won't be any air mattresses! Be faithful. Sow seed. We started at the bottom....humility!
#we2b14ever #countdownto10 #2friends

Teisha's Takeaway

Even though we come from different backgrounds and had different upbringings, we understood that we both brought something unique to the union. We took our differences as an opportunity to learn and understand each other. I was undeniably a spender, and Marcus was clearly a saver. Our previous experiences contributed to the way we manage our finances. We learned quickly that a healthy marriage could consist of a saver and a spender. Yes, there were instances where we thanked God for the wisdom of the saver and times when we thanked God for the gift of the spender. This memory serves as a reminder of God's faithfulness towards us.

We praised God for the new beginning and trusted God to fill the rooms of our house. He has done that not just with our home but with our marriage as well.

Marcus's Takeaway

In Zechariah 4:10, the Bible admonishes us not to despise small beginnings. Teisha and I agreed from day one that we would be more focused on God and the part of us that people couldn't see than the visible components that would be displayed, like houses, cars, furniture, and decor. When she was alright with temporarily sleeping on an inflatable mattress for a short season, I knew she was a woman after my own heart. (LOL). We are very humble and highly grateful for our modest beginning as it aided in setting a solid foundation for our belonging to God and each other rather than our earthly belongings. As God has increased our possessions, they are appreciated more because we know who we are. Nothing outside of us makes us who we are. God in us does that, and we are thankful.

Our Takeaway

Sleeping on the air mattress was similar to saying "I do" in a marriage in that both represented a starting point. Just as we filled our natural home one room at a time, God has added wisdom and other precious intangible jewels to our marital house. A couple sowed a dining room set in our lives, and we picked up items from yard sales and thrift stores to complete our decor throughout our home. Likewise, God has sent people across our paths to sow the Word, encouragement, and support into our marriage to make it look nice. Six years ago, we built a lovely home from the ground up. When we moved in, we furnished all five bedrooms, the family room, the keeping room, the sunroom, the formal dining room, the office, and the game room with very little purchasing. In like manner, our humble beginnings in marriage have flourished into an everlasting, intentional love for God and one another. In fact, we often receive compliments about how awesome our marriage and family are and how happy we are. People did not see how we started from the bottom, but they can appreciate the product they see now.

Another thing, we have been told that some people perceive we think we are all that because of what we have in the natural realm. We respond that if you did not say anything when we were sleeping on an air mattress, please hold your commentary about our current possessions. We love where we are in marriage now, partly because we know where God has brought us from. We are not "all that" because of what we own. We are "all that" because of who owns us! To God be the glory!

Your Takeaway

_____

_____

_____

_____

_____

_____

_____

_____

_____

_____

_____

_____

_____

_____

_____

_____

_____

_____

_____

"Beautiful. I love reading about your relationship with God and each other. You remind me that God is faithful, with everlasting mercy and enduring truths ❤."
~Erica Edwards

Marcus Friend
August 26, 2017

Memory #6 of our #countdownto10 : When Teisha Fletcher-Friend and I were dating I had a motorcycle. We used to go for rides with no destination. We would ride to a parking lot or a street with no traffic and park. We would get off of the motorcycle and sit on the curb or just sit on the bike and talk. We would talk about EVERYTHING! Conversation was fun. Just simple dialogue. We shared until our hearts were content and then we'd leave. We laid a good foundation of communication. We didn't realize how essential that foundation would be in our marriage. When we say "Communication is key" it's not just a cliché to us. We thank God for helping us get off to a good start, even when we had no clue. We're still talking, still learning, still growing, still loving...
#countdownto10 #teamFriend #communicationiskey

Marcus's Takeaway

God was working on us regarding communication before we realized it. Talking to and intentionally listening to one another was a frequent practice as we dated. We did not know how important this would be as our relationship progressed into marriage. If we did not know any better, we would think the phrase "communication is key" is exaggerated. However, being in a marital relationship proves it is mandatory, even when it seems redundant. Those talks we had, while our empty motorcycle helmets sat as if they were a part of the audience, would prove crucial practices for the communication test that our lives would demand us to pass later. It may not always be comfortable, but when necessary, we have the know-how in our arsenal of correspondence. We are grateful that it started; it seems like it was before we intended it.

Teisha's Takeaway

Those rides and conversations were priceless. I enjoyed feeling the night breeze and the bugs flying into my helmet shield, or it was the peace I felt just being free to let my guard down or simply free to be me—unjudged! I remember feeling so safe, although riding 85+ mph down dark, empty roads, safe while sitting on the curb, hearing bugs, and killing mosquitos! As I reflect on this memory, I think about the safety I have when I am with Marcus. I had never experienced such freedom and peace. I held it tightly because I never wanted to be without it again. This was the day "I knew!" This is one of the moments that sealed the deal.

Our Takeaway

Communication is challenging, especially for men, because it causes them to peel back the tough guy layers and welcome vulnerability. We learned in our marriage that practicing, talking, and listening about fun, ordinary, everyday topics will help open stubborn doors of dialogue. In a relaxed, stress-free environment, engaging in conversation is much easier. Enough deliberate and routine discussions prepare you for when it is mandatory. In other words, learning to talk about everything makes it easier to talk about anything. Remember, the right atmosphere to do so is always a plus.

Your Takeaway

"I love it. You are so right. Communication is key. Plus,
love and putting God first."
~ Sandy Hillis Steakley

Memory Seven

Teisha Fletcher-Friend
August 26, 2017

Memory #7 with Marcus Friend
It's no secret the love Marcus and I have for good music..On our wedding night, although exhausted we were running off love and desire to never end the night...we rode through Huntsville in a convertible Jaguar(my dream car) and laughed the night away..As the night begin to wind down Marcus had one more surprise for me...Marcus and I did a drop in at the Labor Day festival on the grounds of A&M...the featured band was none other than the SOS band! They invited us up on stage and spoke blessings over our union..fast forward 9 years and 355 days later and who guess whose concert we are at? SOS Band. What a wonderful surprise AGAIN...and though we weren't On stage we were Back stage...shout out to Yolanda Denson #1newsanchor #we2b14ever #countdownto10 #2friends

Teisha's Takeaway

Music has been my go-to for so many things. This was, without a doubt, icing on the cake for me. We could have stayed on stage dancing forever. To be able to capture this moment years later was unforgettable. We danced, sang, and shared in joy all night long. I still hear the band playing "No One Gonna Love You the Way I Do" and "Take Your Time." We knew the lyrics to all the songs, but more importantly, we were committed to the lyrics' message. Even now, with the hustle and bustle of life, we are devoted to taking our time, getting it right, and loving each other.

Marcus's Takeaway

When we were dating, Teisha and I found another shared love of R&B music, especially Ol' School. We found something we both loved and allowed it to be an inspiration to pull us closer together. It seemed like every time the radio came on, we were holding hands and singing. No matter how out of tune we were, the important thing was our hearts were in harmony and on the same sheet of music. So, no wonder it was perfect timing to interrupt our post-reception cruise around town to stop by the concert of one of our favorite bands/groups. It was such a nice gesture for the crowd to give us a hardy and supportive ovation after I (ahem, ahem...clearing my throat) pulled a couple of strings to get us on stage. The lead singer announced us as newlyweds. We embraced the moment and gave a grateful wave, elevating our blissful night a little higher. As fate would have it, I was not the only one pulling strings that night. Teisha has been tugging at my heartstrings ever since, and I must admit, she is a mighty fine musician in my eyes (wink-wink). #stillloving

Our Takeaway

Music has always provided a sensation and has set an atmosphere because that's how God created it. For us, it is not just about the music, per se, but rather the contributions of every instrument and voice coming together to produce a harmonic sound. Similarly, marriage is not just about just having a ring or being able to say, "I's married now!" Instead, it is about bringing both partners' gifts, talents, strengths, and weaknesses together to blend in a way that sings the melody of a blessed and prosperous marriage. The oneness that keeps us in the groove far outweighs the desire to highlight our individual efforts. After all, if the two want to be soloists, they should not form a duet.

Your Takeaway

"I still play the CD that y'all gave the wedding party. I know y'all love music. Love it. Love y'all."
~Kendria Odoms Jones

Marcus Friend
August 28, 2017

Memory #7 in our #countdownto10 : so when we were getting to know each other a conversation surfaced about our pasts...yeah, it just got real! Teisha Fletcher-Friend had dated some people that had me like "Really? Why?" I had a decision to make-- to continue to dwell on her past decisions or make a decision to move forward. I could walk in pride and think "what will people think" or I could decide to not care what they think. I could be consumed by irrelevant thoughts about stuff that can never be changed or I could go follow my heart and bring change. I could've gotten stuck in a chapter of her book that had already been written or I could unite with her and write a new chapter, a new ending, a new book, our book. Well I chose the latter. I decided to move forward, don't worry about what "they" think, follow my heart, write the ending in OUR book. After all, no man, regardless of his dedication and efforts, can change what WAS; he can only play his part in what IS, to determine what will be. (Though that sounds like a sound bite from a noted philosopher, the Holy Spirit just gave me that!) We're pressing FORWARD. We're learning. We're growing. We're loving. #countdownto10 #teamFriend

Marcus's Takeaway

Somehow during life, as we explore relationships, it seems that a lot of weight is put on our partner's past. Whether dating, in a committed relationship, or in a marriage, we must determine how much we will depend on the scales of history. Yes, I absolutely subscribe to someone's past decisions being an indicator of their future. However, we must determine if a person's present is distanced enough from their former life's choices to make you want to look through the front windshield rather than the rearview mirror. I cannot express how glad I am that I did not let Teisha's past forfeit or ruin our future. We all have a past, and most are not proud of it. This new life together far exceeds the old and is improving daily.

Teisha's Takeaway

Bringing up my past came with many risks, but I was prepared for them all. Discussing the past with Marcus made me cringe, but it was my past—my truth. I remember feeling nervous and in disbelief (like I could not believe I was sharing so much, probably too much). As I was divulging my relationship history, I realized I had made poor decisions because of my pain due to the absence of my father. The more pain I released and answered Marcus's questions honestly, the lighter I felt. I was starting to heal and understand the basis for my poor decisions. I was in a counseling session while on a date—go figure! Nevertheless, the push to go beyond the surface benefited us both and sparked a flame that continues to burn in our communication even today.

Our Takeaway

Though our past plays a part in our lives because it is our history, we must contain it so that it doesn't bleed into the now. We learned that moving forward is a delicate process. We must lightly tread while avoiding judgment as we gather strength to resist being tied to our past. The most challenging form of multitasking is looking backward while proceeding forward. Whether walking, running, riding a bike, driving a vehicle, or pursuing a relationship, it is impossible to constantly maintain a focus ahead and behind without facing disaster. The decision must be made to progress onward, and you must pay attention to what is and will be if you ever move from what was.

Your Takeaway

"Wow! This story tho! It was like a Fairytale of Love!"
~Yolanda Denson

Memory Eight

Teisha Fletcher-Friend
August 29, 2017

#countingdownto10 with Marcus Friend memory #8
When I first met Marcus I did find him attractive. However one of the most defining attributes was his boldness. Marcus has never had a problem expressing his feelings~good or bad~and I admire him for that. But like someone once told me, "the things you love most could possibly be the thing that irritates you later!" Boy was she right....I have tried to quiet Marcus at times while he has tried to get me to speak up at times. Over the years I have found that our opposite attributes are NOT something we should desire to change but instead are what balances our relationship. No longer is my prayer, Lord fix Marcus. Teach him how to be quiet. Show him how to walk and talk with meekness." I now thank the Lord for the gifts he put inside Marcus. And I ask the Lord, "Show me how to accept Marcus for how you created and purposed him!"— with **Marcus Friend**.
#we2b14ever #taleof2friends

Teisha's Takeaway

This memory reminds me of the importance of having balance in our relationship. Having my reserved character and Marcus's direct character has benefited our marriage. I had to identify early that our differences were opportunities for both of us to grow as a couple and as individuals. It was because of Marcus's character that I was able to define and establish some boundaries. I have also become more assertive rather than passive regarding my feelings. So, rather than allowing myself to be irritated with our differences, I have embraced them and utilized them to improve our marriage. I grew here!

Marcus's Takeaway

To maximize the potential and intention of God, we must understand the benefits of what our partners bring to the table in the relationship/marriage. Imagine if they only reflected the same sentiments, thoughts, and ideas that we already have. We would, without a doubt, be bored out of our minds. Furthermore, our growth would be limited and even stunted. We would not be challenged to expand our thinking and welcome the ideas and profound expressions of the other minds in the union. We are where we were weak, and so are our mates. We must fight to keep open minds so we do not miss the help God purposed us to receive from our help mate.

Our Takeaway

Perspective is key as it pertains to what our significant other brings to the table. We must see the value in the adage, "Two heads are better than one." After all, if you were fulfilled, complete, and satisfied with being single and single-minded, then you would not have explored the heart of your other half. Along with their heart comes their mind, including their thoughts, ideas, and perspectives. As we welcome these attributes into our world, we can only become better, wiser, and more complete than what we were absent from them. This brings life to the familiar saying, "We are better together."

Your Takeaway

"So sweet"
~Darlene Pride

Marcus Friend
August 31, 2017 · 🌐

Memory #8 in my #countdownto10 : a few years ago Teisha Fletcher-Friend and I had a disagreement. We weren't seeing eye to eye concerning what to do about transportation. We had two vehicles and one was broken and in the shop. Thus, I arranged our schedule for us to leave earlier, drop kids off, drop me off at work which meant she had to sit at work 30-60 minutes before her shift started, I had to wait around to be picked up so forth and so on. To me it was a minor inconvenience. To her, all this shuffling around and rearranging was "stupid" because the solution was simple, we could just borrow her brother's car and be done with it. I was raised for years in a single parent home that had NO car. I was raised being taught that the man is the provider. I was raised not to depend on others unless you absolutely HAD to. She was raised in a home where there was always a car. She was raised and taught that that's what family is for (to help). She thought, why go through unnecessary changes when help is available? Neither of our perspectives was "right or wrong"...just different. It became a big deal. I was grateful for the one car we had. She couldn't understand what was so hard about using someone else's car. In the end, she borrowed her brother's car and I asked her to give it back. She did but then there was attitude. (This got ugly y'all!) I told her that as a man, I would not use another person's stuff when all it took was a lil sacrifice. I asked her her to just respect my decision. She did but it wasn't easy! After about a week our 2nd car was fixed. That was a major learning experience for us. Lesson: the two shall become one. Even, if they don't agree someone has to be the leader and delegated authority. In our home, it's me. I consider my wife's wishes, my family's well being and our safety but in the end the RESPONSIBILITY for my family falls on me. We're not just going to run for help and wave the white flag when we don't have to. Since then my wife respects my decisions a lot better, knowing that I consider her input as well. We didn't just GET here we GREW here. NOW you see why we celebrate! Still learning, still growing, still loving. #countdownto10 #teamFriend #wegrewhere

Marcus's Takeaway

One thing that is so clear is when the two become one, we are attempting to merge two different backgrounds and upbringings into one household, all while trying to discover what from each person's bag of experience works best for the scenario that we are currently facing. It is perfectly permissible to mesh mindsets, but at the same time, we must set some solid boundaries. For instance, while presenting each one's case for why their point of view is valid, there must be a way to agree on a final resolution, even if both parties still have different opinions. In this instance, I'm responsible for paying the bills, providing transportation, having what we need to survive, and so on. Thus, I did not want to introduce the idea that we resort to an outside entity if we were inconvenienced. Lord knows I have the best brother-in-law in the world, but I was not ready for my family to depend on him to provide anything unnecessary. If it becomes one, then I, as the man of the house and head of the family, would go to him (or whoever) to make the accommodations. Of all the presentations on our countdown to ten, I venture to say this was the experience where we learned the most. We used our resources from the couple's group we are a part of and our mentor couple whom we designated to help us resolve issues. In the end, I respect and value my wife's input. She allows me to serve my purpose as the provider, even if we must sacrifice more than usual. I promise to love and provide the best for her, and she promises to trust me to do just that. All is well in this area now, but believe me when I say we grew here!

Teisha's Takeaway

Wow! What another defining moment in our relationship! If trying to resolve the car issue wasn't enough, I regretfully continued to add fuel to the fire with my careless words.... "This is so stupid!" Thank God for wise counsel. We were able to compromise and work together to resolve the transportation issue. Still, we also had to self-check to keep our pride and ego from escalating the situation. Looking back, I can now see how I subconsciously thought my way was right; therefore, his way had to be wrong. How selfish and/or self-centered my thoughts were! How quickly something so simple spiraled out of control. Well, several years later, I appreciate this memory. We both have different strategies for approaching issues. Because we had different upbringings, our approach to resolving conflicts may not be wrong; it is simply different. Differences are okay when we learn to respect them and work together to navigate "our way."

Our Takeaway

There are going to be challenging moments in every union. The best wisdom we can offer is to pray and have a plan when these challenges arise. Stick with the plan so emotions will not overpower logic in your decision-making. We didn't have a plan for what we would do if we were ever down to one vehicle. Thus, two different points of view clashed when we needed to make a desperate decision. This resulted in frustration, misunderstanding, and poor choices of words while pursuing solutions. We both thought that position was the way to go. We both had good ideas but were pretty different, and we could not do both. Sacrificing and getting out of your routine when you don't have to is just as frustrating as the feeling of not being heard. Yet, we had to decide. We both acquired much more knowledge about each other than we thought we already knew. "Communication is key" is an understatement here. We learned many valuable lessons: develop a plan, execute the plan, prepare for difficult moments, respect each other's perspectives, love and respect each other amid challenges, season your words with love, keep a reliable support system, and so much more. This experience was a doozy, y'all, but we survived, loved, learned, and grew!

Your Takeaway

_____

_____

_____

_____

_____

_____

_____

_____

_____

_____

_____

_____

_____

_____

_____

_____

_____

_____

_____

"Through you two, others are inspired and educated on the reality of marriage. Your insight showed the good, the bad, the ugly, and the COMMITMENT that it takes to endure. You guys are a blessing."
~Crystal Mitchell

Memory Nine

Teisha Fletcher-Friend
August 31, 2017

Memory #9 with Marcus Friend....
There's no secret that Marcus and I have had our "trying times" but we have endured through them...Not because we learned how to play the blame game or should I say not because we know everything. I attribute our steadfastness to God. I remember visiting several churches before we got married. Although we both had our home church, we wanted a place to grow together where I wasn't known as Marcus' wife and he wasn't referred to as Teisha's husband. We were at two different places in our walk with the Lord but we both wanted MORE...finally, the week of our wedding we visited Church of the Firstborn Christian Center and we both received confirmation that this was our new home. As a couple, find a church that teaches the Word; one that will build your character; one that holds you accountable! When the enemy comes in..you will need a Word~not entertainment~to build up a standard(for your marriage). This like all other memories is to encourage you to seek God. A marriage built on anything other than God's Word WILL NOT make it! Pray together. Study the Word together. Seek God together..
#countingdownto10 #we2b14ever

Teisha's Takeaway

I confess that our relationship would not be what it is today without 1) a solid personal relationship with Christ and 2) a community of like-minded believers who undergirded us with the truth of God's love. Uniting as one can be difficult, so establishing and maintaining a community with sound doctrine is critical. Respecting the call or anointing on your partner's life is much easier when you both know and believe the Word. Yes, we both were believers in Christ, but we were not disciplined and did not have the same encounters. Now that we have been studying, counseling, and worshipping God together under the same leadership, we and our marriage have matured. We face and conquer obstacles together according to the Word of God. I am not saying our marriage is perfect, but because we seek God together, we are definitely stronger and more united.

Marcus's Takeaway

Undoubtedly, God must be at the foundation of every marriage to survive and thrive. Teisha and I agreed, which made finding a church home together easier. We prayed and were led to where we could establish our own identity as a family. Later, as our family grew, it was built on the solid rock, Jesus Christ, and His kingdom principles. Despite the difficulties and challenges, we have always believed in God to sustain us, show us how to manage life, and be with us through it all. We've always been proud of how our spiritual walk started together, and we're still pleased with where and how God continues to lead us now. We began in Him, grew in Him, learned in Him, and love in Him.

Our Takeaway

Every married couple should know God instituted, implemented, and ordained marriage. Therefore, the expectation should be that because He established it, He should not only be in it but also guide it. When you take the Creator out of the thing He created, chaos is inevitable. Consequently, it is crucial that every couple, even considering marriage, pursue it God's way. It's just as vital to follow the model He outlined in His Word. For example, a man will find his wife. He will love her as Christ loves the church. She will submit to His leadership and covering. She will support him. He will provide for her. He will protect her. The two shall become one. When we do it His way, we can expect His results. We must realize that Godly success and results are not guaranteed unless we do it according to His Word. However, the world may offer different ways, and various results come with that. Of course, we do not advocate in any way other than God's! Seek God together, pray together, establish Godly standards, and join in faith together so that God will stamp His approval of "good" on your marriage. We are so glad we knew to do this from the beginning, and we indeed emphasize to you how imperative it is to do this as well. There is nothing like God's standard of "good" because with His approval comes His blessings.

Your Takeaway

"I swear you two are my favorite young couple and you inspire single people that real love exists. I love you!"
~Tanisha D. Smith

Marcus Friend
September 1, 2017

Memory #9 in our #countdownto10 : Teisha Fletcher-Friend and I established early in our marriage that "divorce was not an option!" We said that word would not even be mentioned in our home. It was uttered one time and I won't say by who but she promised not to say it again...lol. But seriously, we have had to work hard to keep our marriage healthy and functioning properly. Many people told us "Marraige is what you make it." Others warned, "Marriage is hard work." We found both to be true. I would like to present another perspective. I will parallel marraige to a road from it's conception. When the idea is conceived (proposal) it's met with the joys of how nice and convenient and beautiful it can and will be. The hard work with developing a road starts ('I do') when the trees and even rocks/mountains (traditions, opinions from others, ideologies, etc) have to be carved through and cut down. Once those are removed a solid dirt foundation (God) must be laid firm. Upon it must be gravel, rock, and other hard durable sustances (love, trust, forgiveness, support, loyalty, faithfulness, etc.). Then when all of that is done, the asphalt tops it off nice with white and/or yellow lines that makes the part that people see really look nice. People drive on the fresh clean pavement (see you joyfully loving one another) but don't see the dirt that's supporting it and making it possible to exist. There are many layers that contribute to it's beauty and strength. Even after the heavy equipment (wedding/honeymoon) has served it's purpose, there must be maintenance (conferences, date nights, fellowship with other couples, alone time, etc) throughout the duration of the life of it in order for it to reach it's full potential and longevity. It's easy to spot a bumpy road with dips and potholes. When we ride on them we often complain and sometimes detour. We should be just as sensitive to the uncomfortable ride in our marriage. Sometimes it may require digging back down to the foundation in order to fix it. Whatever it takes to keep our ride smooth, I'm willing to do. Whatever it takes to keep the 'd' word out of our lives forever. We will NOT detour! (or the other 'd' word either!) Still learning, still growing, still loving. #countdownto10 #teamFriend #wegrewhere

Marcus's Takeaway

Let me just emphatically state I thank God for flowing in us through the Holy Spirit because this analogy blessed my soul! We must understand that there are many layers of marriage. Just as people are multifaceted, complex individuals, it would be foolish to think that you can merge two different, complicated, elaborate lives, and it results in a simplistic, effortless cakewalk of a marriage. We must deliberate about discovery and acknowledge that every person and marriage is different. Don't be afraid to retract the coverings that tend to veil the heart. We tend to see this as a negative, but good things are hidden there, too. Sometimes, the spot on the outside of the fruit indicates a problem at the core. Dig and plow, plow and dig until you reach that firm foundation and realize He is solid, and then your marriage can be as well. Don't ever be so low that you cannot enjoy the beauty of the asphalt. Similarly, don't be so high that you forget what you are built on. A healthy marriage is something that you must build! Yes, the wedding and honeymoon will be memorable, but the participants must be willing to invest in the marriage for it to prosper. Invest time. Invest in dates. Invest prayer. Invest in getaways. Invest support. Invest in intimate moments. Invest sacrifice. Invest determination. In turn, you will assuredly reap what you sow. Most people will look at your nuptial tree and see beautiful fruit. Few know the tilling, digging, planting, and especially watering and fertilizing involved. That is okay because you don't do it for people; you do it for longevity in a successful and fulfilling union. Is marriage hard work? Sometimes. Is marriage what you make it? Most certainly. The question we must all ask ourselves is, "Is it worth it?" Our answer should always be a resounding- "You better believe it!"

Teisha's Takeaway

This is where I had to decide if I was really willing to do the tough work of making our marriage healthy and successful. The first years of our marriage were hard for me because it would not be so difficult to uproot a lot of misinformation and the fairytale ideal of marriage. Truthfully, in our first years of marriage, I realized I did not know much, but I did know I wanted a forever relationship built on love and respect for each other. So, I put on my boots and allowed the Holy Spirit to guide and mentor me through the work. Our road has been bumpy sometimes, but we did what was necessary to smooth things over. Oftentimes, we as women get so hypnotized by the magic of planning a wedding that we minimize or even disregard the marriage. Yes, I said it. The wedding and the marriage are two different things. However, without the proper attention to the marriage, the wedding is just for show. I am so thankful for the preparation and maintenance we give to our marriage, so I would never speak that "D" word again.

Our Takeaway

In today's world of social media boasting, filled with the glamor of beautiful pictures and broadcasted victories, many couples spend way more time, energy, and money preparing for the wedding than they do for the marriage. This misguided layout emphasizes the looks on the surface rather than the framework of the union, which often goes neglected. Then, when the wedding dress is hung in the closet, the tuxedos have been returned to the local formal wear rental merchant, and the suitcases from the honeymoon have been unpacked and stashed away, that is when the proverbial rubber meets the road. Without proper counseling and preparation, disaster (and the other D word) can present itself as an easy out. That is why it is key to prohibit the nasty "D" word from your conversation and your options well before it knocks on the door of your marital home. The Bible says, in Isaiah 59:19, "When the enemy comes in like a flood, the Lord will lift up a standard against him." In 100% of marriages, the enemy has reared his ugly head to try to implement the spirit of division in one way or another. Tests and trials are inevitable; nevertheless, victory lies in your resources: from Godly wisdom to sound teaching, to faith, to wise counsel, and beyond. The tools for a healthy marriage are available. The husband and wife must apply themselves to attain and utilize them. In other words, don't be deceived into thinking that your marriage will ride on a smooth, prefabricated road with no curves, hills, potholes, or speed bumps. Rest assured that you will make it through if God is leading and guiding you. Though each marriage is unique to the individuals that make it up, one common factor that they all have is that they require a calculated effort by both parties to flourish. So, stay the course, do the work, and keep the "D" word out of range so that it never reaches our address. #wegrewhere For real!

Your Takeaway

"That was good. I will share."
~Markita Friend

Memory Ten

Teisha Fletcher-Friend
September 4, 2017

The final #countdownto10 memory with Marcus Friend...Earlier in our marriage Marcus and I approached a fork in the road...if the truth be told, it was a decision I was going to have to make that would expose my willingness to submit. Marc told me "stick with me I'll show you some things and take you some places"! In my mind I thought that was very arrogant and was even offensive. Does he think I'm not capable of seeing without him or going without him? He really is arrogant and if nothing else I'll show him I can do somethings and think without him. Obviously I had subconsciously reverted back to my "single mindset" and was preparing to rebuild walls that I knew would separate us..Was it really worth it? What I thought was a problem for Marcus was actually God revealing issues within me. I really had a problem with submission (aka control issues) and it was going to be an opportunity to either grow or remain stagnant because of my pride... Whether single or married I realized that if I didn't learn how to submit I was NEVER going to grow! Reality check: I was having a problem submitting to Marcus bc I really hadn't submitted to the Lord! Well here we are 10 years later and I'm seeing things I haven't seen and going places I've never been only because I surrendered to God and His way of doing things.
Lesson: Embrace the rewards of submitting to God~better vision. expanded territory.
#countdownto10 #teamfriend #we2b14ever

Teisha's Takeaway

Truth can be an extremely hard yet rewarding pill to swallow. The truth is I struggled with relinquishing control. In my mind, I had made it far by doing it my way. I thought, "Who in the world does he think he is?" Oh boy, does God know how to reveal the issues of our hearts. I would miss my blessing if I did not allow God to heal this hidden area. So, it may have sounded like an arrogant statement, but it propelled me into a deeper relationship with God. As strong and independent women, we must know that submission is not a weakness but a sign of strength. Anyone can take charge and do as they feel; true strength is measured in self-control and obedience–obedience to God's truth. So yes, Marcus has shown me much, and he has taken me to different places, and I thank him; despite that, if I did not allow God to work on my submission, I would not be experiencing that expansion of my spiritual tent pegs.

Marcus's Takeaway

If you are not careful and prayerful, you can reject the very thing sent to bless you. I wanted to take Teisha to places and experience things that she nor I had ever encountered. When I expressed that to her, the last thing I wanted was resistance. I wanted her to embrace the journey. I wanted her to stick with me through thick and thin. Though we might not have traveled the world, partaking in diverse cultures within the first year or two, we would eventually. I also desired for her to see that my statement could have just as well applied to marriage in general and not only traveling. For instance, I hoped she would go deeper in her relationship with God. I wanted her to see that nothing could stop us if we did what we needed to keep our marriage thriving. So, when I said, "You'll go some places and see some things," I can say with surety she has on many levels, and so have I. I am happy she took down the wall and decided to enjoy the ride. It is, without question, one worth engaging in.

Our Takeaway

So many times, people get stuck because they will not deal with their hidden issues. It will be difficult moving forward if we do not peel back the layers and deal with them. Picture a hot-air balloon that is tied and anchored down. It does not matter how much helium is released into the inside of it; it will not rise. In life, we can be tied and anchored down in our pasts and with our old mindsets, as exhibited when that statement was made in the post. Reverting to the old way of thinking prohibits growth on several levels. When one does submit to God's way and begin to see through His eyes, the ropes are cut, and the anchor is severed. Only then can they see the situation differently. We have traveled somewhere every year for our anniversary. In fact, we are currently sitting beachside enjoying a constant ocean breeze that feels about seventy degrees as we put the final additions on our first book, *When Two Become One: Our Transparent Journey of Experiences that Shaped the Foundation of Our Marriage.* We are so free: no strings, no ropes, no anchors!

Your Takeaway

"I will join my faith with your faith that God will bless you with many more years of wedding bliss. When you keep Him first, everything else falls in place."
~Annie Readus-Erskine

Marcus Friend
September 3, 2017

Memory #10 of our #countdownto10 : This is the last one in this series. I remember standing at the altar looking my gorgeous bride, Teisha Fletcher-Friend, in the eyes and repeating our vows and listening to the officiants. One in particular, "...and the two shall become one" was more sound bite than reality at the time. Most often, couples don't REALLY understand that one. Becoming one, as we have grown, means whatever state one was in, the other is drafted in immediately! For instance, I'm a stickler for financial freedom and responsibility. I DID NOT want $65,000 of student loan debt, another car payment, another house payment, etc. However, her debt became my debt. Her responsibility became mine. She and I became ONE! Teisha, as she mentioned in one of her memories, wasn't looking for a ready made family which meant taking on a PERMANENT parenting roll on day one. She and I became ONE. It's was no longer "his" and "hers", it became "ours"- our debt, our responsibility, our child, our issues, our money, our vision, our cars, our house(s), our, our, OUR. 'For better or for worse' indicates that 'ours' may not always be what we want, it may very well be what we don't want. However, "the two shall become one." To this day, if truth be told, that is a struggle in more marriages than not. I encourage all married readers of this message to take on what your spouse brought and work together. We, only by the GRACE of God, have become ONE. We haven't arrived at perfection but we love perfectly- with all that we have because when you love your spouse, you love yourself! We are ONE. We are still learning, still growing, still loving... #countdownto10 #teamFriend #wegrewhere #byGodsgrace

Marcus's Takeaway

Marriage is the most unselfish institution men and women can enter. If this principle of sacrificing, sharing, and preferring the other is not understood and adhered to, there will be many long days and sleepless nights. The most sobering piece of advice that I can give someone considering marriage is, "It is not about you!" Being self-centered is never a good characteristic of a marriage partner. Each spouse must acknowledge that their way may not be the best or the best at that time. A healthy marriage requires being open-minded. If you want everything to go your way, you might as well stay single. On day one, what's yours is theirs, and what's theirs is yours, like it or not. Since the two are becoming one, two mindsets merge to point in the same direction, not one domineering voice. My dear reader, this is the most crucial skill to master in marriage.

Teisha's Takeaway

This memory is the totality of marriage, learning to dissolve the "my" and embrace the "our" mentality and concept. It is easy to identify with "our" when it's what you want or benefit from joining, but it can be challenging when "our" doesn't appear favorable. It is simple when it is "our" income, but becoming "our" debt is difficult. For some, the concept is defined as mine, theirs, and ours. Marcus and I trusted the "one" ideology and relied on God to manifest it. Was it challenging? Yes, of course, but it was worth it. We learned that although we had different approaches to mastering things, it did not mean one was right or wrong. Instead, developing "our" way became the focus. Uniting two ways of life required a team approach. The focus was and continues to be one. So, when people say you lost yourself in the marriage, I consider that a positive; the idea is to lose yourself and become one!

Our Takeaway

The two shall become one. This statement sounds so simple, yet it is the most profound statement in traditional marriage vows. There are so many aspects of life that become one. Everything from debt, children, finances, name, identity, life goals, vision, mindset, and decision-making to faith, family, direction, and more are affected. When a marriage breaks down, it is because there is an area where the two did not or have not become one. The question is, how do you define "oneness?" We, #teamFriend, view oneness as being like a jigsaw puzzle. The husband brings his pieces, and the wife brings her pieces. At the altar, they begin to piece them together. Every piece, whether his or hers, has its place. As the pieces come together, the picture they form is not his or hers but rather theirs. The picture must become one solid, undivided masterpiece of togetherness. The whole thing belongs to both parties equally. Each one contributed and surrendered everything they had to interlock with the other. Now, when anyone sees the finished product, it is ONE.!Family members cannot separate it. Friends, especially single ones, cannot separate it. The past cannot separate it. This is why it is paramount to get to know your potential spouse; once you become one, you are one! Not even the husband and/or wife are supposed to put asunder what God put together. This wisdom will help engaged couples realize marriage starts after the cute wedding ceremony ends. Always invest more in the marriage than in the wedding. Prepare for all your spouse's stuff (wanted and unwanted) to be yours on day one. You can't take their income while rejecting their debt. You can't receive the benefits and favor of their position but not contribute to or support their vision. Two becoming one means you are on the same page, following the same game plan, moving in the same direction, marching to the same beat, with the same mindset, and striving to achieve goals together. The two becoming one might not be the easiest objective, but it will benefit your marriage the most. When you

master this, you can definitely #keepgrowing
#keeplearning #keeploving.

Your Takeaway

"I love y'all!!!!"
NikkiLarue Leland

Made in the USA
Columbia, SC
17 March 2025